X-TREME FACTS: NATURAL DISASTERS

Extreme Heat and Droughts

by Marcia Abramson

BEARPORT PUBLISHING

Minneapolis, Minnesota

Credits:

Title Page, 15 top right, Bits And Splits/Shutterstock; 4 top, Michael Vi/Shutterstock.com; 4 top left, fizkes/Shutterstock; 4 top right, Blackwhitepailyn/Shutterstock; 4 bottom, Sergii Figurnyi/Shutterstock; 5 top, A_Lesik/Shutterstock;5 top left, tab62/Shutterstock; 5 top right, QBR/Shutterstock; 5 middle, Sergey Krasnoshchokov/Shutterstock; 5 bottom left, Marcella Miriello/Shutterstock; 5 bottom right, milosk50/Shutterstock; 5 middle left, Dorindavidaurel/Creative Commons; 5 middle right, nikitich viktoriya/Shutterstock.com; 6 NOAA/Public Domain; 6 bottom right, Sergey Novikov/Shutterstock; 7 top, Andocs/Shutterstock.com 7 top right, Prostock-studio/Shutterstock; 7 bottom, rblfmr/Shutterstock.com; 7 bottom left, 9 bottom right, 21 top left, 23 top right, 25 bottom middle, 26 top right, 26 bottom, LightField Studios/Shutterstock; 7 bottom right, Naveen Macro/Shutterstock.com; 8 top, Petr Baumann/Shutterstock; 8 bottom, Sumit Saraswat/Shutterstock.com; 8 bottom left, Westock Productions/Shutterstock; 8 bottom right, Indian concepts/Shutterstock; 9 top, eddtoro/Shutterstock.com; 9 top left, Steve Sanchez Photos/Shutterstock.com; 9 bottom, ssguy/Shutterstock; 9 bottom left, paffy/Shutterstock; 10, New Africa/Shutterstock; 11 top, PR Image Factory/Shutterstock; 11 middle, 3 Dias Fotografia/Shutterstock; 11 middle left, Lester Balajadia/Shutterstock;com; 11 middle right, Alexisrael/Creative Common; 11 bottom, Kristesoro/Shutterstock; 11 bottom right, Firn/Shutterstock; 12 top, AmeliAU/Shutterstock; 12 bottom, dropStock/Shutterstock; 13 top, Anna Kornak/Shutterstock; 13 middle, Somchai Som/Shutterstock; 13 bottom, Dani Llao Calvet/Shutterstock; 14, ESO/S. Brunier/Creative Commons; 14 left, 14 right, Design Projects/Shutterstock; 14 middle, Lucy.Brown/Shutterstock.com; 15 top left, AlexandrMusuc/Shutterstock; 15 top middle, Bits And Splits/Shutterstock; 15 top right, Bits And Splits/Shutterstock; 15 bottom, paulista/Shutterstock; 15 bottom left, Paul Hermans/Creative Commons; 15 bottom middle, Gorodenkoff/Shutterstock; 15 bottom right, Denis---S/Shutterstock; 16-17 top, Vineyard Perspective/Shutterstock; 16 bottom, U.S. National Archives and Records Administration/Public Domain; 16 middle, Dorothea Lange/Public Domain; 17 top, NOAA George E. Marsh Album, theb1365, Historic C&GS Collection/Public Domain; 17 bottom, ModernNomads/Shutterstock.com; 17 bottom left, Jeka/Shutterstock;17 bottom right, maroke/Shutterstock; 18 top, 19 top, Viacheslav Lopatin/Shutterstock; 18 bottom, Leslie Foot/Shutterstock; 18 bottom left, Luis Cristofori/Shutterstock; 18 bottom right, StudioSmart/Shutterstock; 19 bottom, icemanphotos/Shutterstock; 19 bottom middle, Karel Bock/Shutterstock; 19 bottom right, Robert Eastman/Shutterstock; 20 top, Deyan Georgiev/Shutterstock; 20 bottom, Alex Ionas/Shutterstock; 20 bottom right, gianni31 joker/Shutterstock; 20 bottom middle, Edgar G Biehle/Shutterstock; 20 bottom left, Artur_Sarkisyan/Shutterstock; 21 top, Nadya Kubik/Shutterstock; 21 top right, BearFotos/Shutterstock; 21 bottom left, shuttermuse/Shutterstock; 21 bottom middle, Somchai Som/Shutterstock; 21 bottom right, jo Crebbin/Shutterstock; 22, Gorodenkoff/Shutterstock; 22 right, fizkes/Shutterstock; 23 top, Creative Lab/Shutterstock; 23 top left, BearFotos/Shutterstock; 23 bottom, Serhii Fedoruk/Shutterstock; 23 bottom left, nimito/Shutterstock; 23 bottom middle, Jim Barber/Shutterstock; 23 bottom right, Roman Samborskyi/Shutterstock; 24 top, Anton Dios/Shutterstock; 24 bottom, Andrei Armiagov/Shutterstock; 24 bottom left, Gorodenkoff/Shutterstock; 25 top, Monkey Business Images/Shutterstock; 25 middle, Lucas Eduardo Benetti/Shutterstock; 25 bottom, Golden Dayz/Shutterstock; 25 bottom left, Oxyman/Creative Commons; 25 bottom right, Hellotica/Shutterstock.com; 26 top, antoniodiaz/Shutterstock; 27 top, PT Hamilton/Shutterstock; 27 top left, LifetimeStock/Shutterstock; 27 top right, Jeka/Shutterstock; 27 middle, SergeMelkovart/Shutterstock; 27 bottom, Tapui/Shutterstock; 28 top left, Luigi Bertello/Shutterstock; 28 bottom left, Tompix/Shutterstock; 28-29, Austen Photography

Bearport Publishing Company Product Development Team

President: Jen Jenson; Director of Product Development: Spencer Brinker; Managing Editor: Allison Juda; Associate Editor: Naomi Reich; Associate Editor: Tiana Tran; Senior Designer: Colin O'Dea; Associate Designer: Elena Klinkner; Associate Designer: Kayla Eggert; Product Development Specialist: Anita Stasson

Produced for Bearport Publishing by BlueAppleWorks Inc.

Managing Editor for BlueAppleWorks: Melissa McClellan
Art Director: T.J. Choleva
Photo Research: Jane Reid

Library of Congress Cataloging-in-Publication Data is available at www.loc.gov or upon request from the publisher.

ISBN: 979-8-88509-979-0 (hardcover)
ISBN: 979-8-88822-159-4 (paperback)
ISBN: 979-8-88822-299-7 (ebook)

Copyright © 2024 Bearport Publishing Company. All rights reserved. No part of this publication may be reproduced in whole or in part, stored in any retrieval system, or transmitted in any form or by any means, electronic, mechanical, photocopying, recording, or otherwise, without written permission from the publisher.

For more information, write to Bearport Publishing, 5357 Penn Avenue South, Minneapolis, MN 55419.

Contents

Dry as Dust 4

Under Pressure 6

Waves Worldwide 8

Unhealthy Heat 10

Stopping the Cycle 12

Determining Drought 14

Dust and Devastation 16

Weird Waves 18

The Human Element 20

Science to the Rescue 22

Be Prepared! 24

A Cool Future 26

Too Salty! 28

Glossary 30

Read More 31

Learn More Online 31

Index 32

About the Author 32

Dry as Dust

After a long, hot summer, people are getting worried. The sun scorches from high in the sky as the thermometer inches upward. The public pool is closed as the city tries to save water. And at the nearby farms, most of the crops have withered and died. The land is so dry that every passing wind sends the dusty soil flying through the air. Is there any relief in sight from this dreaded heat wave and devastating drought?

A heat wave is a period of unusually hot weather that lasts at least several days.

Heat waves can stretch on for several weeks, often with little or no rain.

Prolonged heat waves can often lead to droughts, **which are drier than normal conditions.**

Since 2000, parts of the western United States have been experiencing the worst drought in 1,200 years.

In cold regions, there can be snow droughts. An unusually small amount of snowfall can stretch for months.

Droughts and heat waves can change history. **Extreme droughts may have contributed to the collapse of the ancient Egyptian and Mayan empires.**

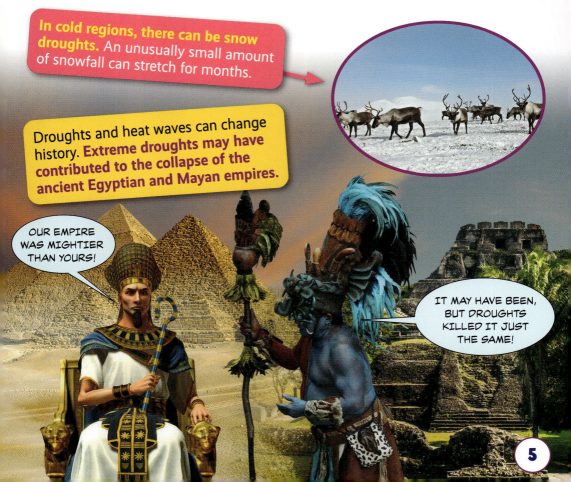

Under Pressure

A heat wave starts in the air above Earth. High pressure moves into an area and pushes warm air down to the surface. As the air sinks, it gets even hotter and drier. A lack of moisture prevents any clouds from forming. A cloudless sky means more sunlight can beat down, raising temperatures further.

Summer weather patterns change less quickly than winter ones, so all that heat-causing pressure can stick around for days or even weeks.

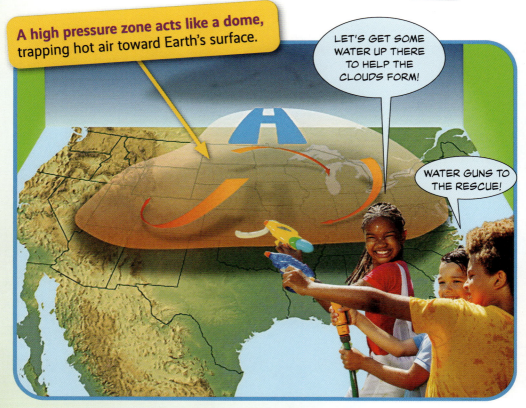

A high pressure zone acts like a dome, trapping hot air toward Earth's surface.

LET'S GET SOME WATER UP THERE TO HELP THE CLOUDS FORM!

WATER GUNS TO THE RESCUE!

As high pressure domes warm the earth, they get rid of moisture near the ground so it can't rise up and form clouds.

The surfaces of roads and buildings soak up sunlight and then give off extra heat in a way that grassy fields do not. It's hotter in the city!

Record high temperatures now happen twice as often as record lows in the United States.

Waves Worldwide

Heat waves hit places that are typically warm. But they don't spare the colder parts of the world, either. Siberia, in Russia, is known for its bitterly cold winters. But in 2020, it experienced a 6-month-long heat wave, with temperatures rising above 100 degrees Fahrenheit (38 degrees Celsius). Likewise, the Pacific Northwest usually enjoys mild temperatures year round. But in 2021, it experienced a record-shattering heat wave. The temperature hit 116°F (47°C) in Portland, Oregon.

Heat waves can cause train tracks to buckle and warp out of shape.

A 2015 heat wave in India caused some streets to melt!

During heat waves, many communities open public cooling centers where people can enjoy free water and air conditioning.

In some places, firefighters may open up hydrants so kids can cool off in the refreshing water.

Sidewalks can get hot enough to fry an egg, but don't eat your breakfast from the sidewalk! An egg won't cook completely, and you could get sick.

SHOULD WE TRY THIS STREET-FRIED EGG?

Plan on flying to escape the heat? Many airplanes are grounded when the temperature gets over 120°F (49°C).

NO, THANKS. I LIKE MY EGGS WELL DONE.

Unhealthy Heat

For people not lucky enough to have air conditioning, heat waves can be extremely harmful. On hot days, our bodies sweat. As this moisture on our skin **evaporates**, it cools us down. But in hot, **humid** weather, sweat doesn't evaporate as quickly, so our bodies start to overheat. It is easy to become **dehydrated** when we get very hot. Too much heat can make us very sick. Signs of heat-related sicknesses include headaches, muscle cramps, weakness, dizziness, an upset stomach, and vomiting.

Extreme heat is one of the leading causes of weather-related deaths in the United States.

When a person's body temperature rises over 104°F (40°C), they have **heatstroke**. This can damage organs and may even be deadly.

An important way to stay healthy during a heat wave is to drink lots of water. Eat foods that have lots of water in them, too!

Heat illness can make people see things. **Tennis player Frank Dancevic said he saw the cartoon character Snoopy on court while playing during a heat wave!**

Pets can get heatstroke, too! Give them lots of water and a cool place to stay.

Stopping the Cycle

Heat waves can cause even more trouble when they trigger droughts. This is a period of time when there is less than the normal amount of precipitation in an area. Typically, the water cycle keeps water moving through an environment from the soil and water on land, up to the sky as clouds, then back down as rain and snow. During a heat wave, high pressure dries the air as it heats up. This prevents the formation of clouds, which stops rainfall.

Because of the water cycle, we are drinking some of the same water dinosaurs slurped!

Plants normally help keep water moving through the water cycle. But they can't take up water during a drought.

If we use a lot of water on our lawns, in our pools, or during long showers, **we may not have enough to get us through heat waves and droughts.**

Our planet is covered in water, but most of it is ocean water. Unfortunately, this salty water cannot be used for many human needs during a drought.

SORRY, FOLKS!

Several batches of soaking rainfall over a few months can end a drought. They replenish **groundwater** that feeds streams and keeps plants alive during dry periods.

A drought is only truly over when typical precipitation and water levels return to normal.

13

Determining Drought

Different parts of the globe expect different levels of annual precipitation. Some regions are rained on most days of the year, while other areas may receive little more than a few drops of water. That means although one area may get more rain than another, it could still be in a drought! It all has to do with the expected rain or snowfall in each place.

The Indian town of Mawsynram typically has about 40 feet (12 m) of rain a year. **Even if it received 20 ft (6 m) one year, it would still be considered in a drought.**

The Atacama Desert in Chile gets an average of only 0.03 inches (0.08 cm) of rainfall a year. As long as it has that much rain, it's not in a drought.

The Maria Elena South area of the Atacama Desert is as dry as Mars!

Dust and Devastation

Droughts are a big threat that can lead to further disasters. Without water, **vegetation** in a region starts to dry and die. If lightning strikes, it can spark wildfires that burn and spread quickly when fueled by the dry plants. Crop plants are often also affected by droughts. If farmers can't water them enough, our food crops die, leading to hunger and **famine**. Loose, dry soil left behind in fields can be blown into serious dust storms that threaten the lives of people and other animals in an area.

One of the worst droughts in history stretched from 1876 until 1879. The resulting famine killed as many as 13 million people in China.

Throughout the 1930s, the usually green and **fertile** Great Plains became so dry they were nicknamed the Dust Bowl.

IT'S LOOKING A LITTLE DRY OUT THERE.

THAT'S WHY THEY CALL IT THE DUST BOWL!

During the serious drought of the 1930s, huge clouds of dried-out soil blocked the sun, made it difficult to breathe, and spread diseases.

Strong winds carried these dust clouds as far as 2,000 miles (3,200 km)!

In 2022, Europe experienced its worst series of heat waves and droughts in 500 years. Rivers dried up, crops died, and wildfires broke out.

In 2012, two-thirds of the lower 48 states were drought-stricken.

OUR RIVER IS ALMOST GONE!

WHAT DO YOU EXPECT IN SUCH TERRIBLE HEAT?

17

Weird Waves

Some heat waves and droughts can be expected. Every few years, a weather pattern called El Niño forms. Waters in the eastern Pacific become unusually warm, and low pressure moves in. At the same time, high pressure develops in the western Pacific. All this changes the direction and strength of winds, steering weather where it wouldn't normally go. La Niña is the opposite. In this pattern, the eastern Pacific cools, creating a chain reaction of unusual weather across the globe.

El Niño brings milder winters to the Northern United States and Canada, drier weather to Hawaii and the Western United States, and wetter conditions to the Gulf states.

When ocean life such as corals are struck by **unusual weather patterns from El Niño, they can get sick or die.**

WHAT HAPPENED TO THE CORALS?

EL NIÑO HAPPENED.

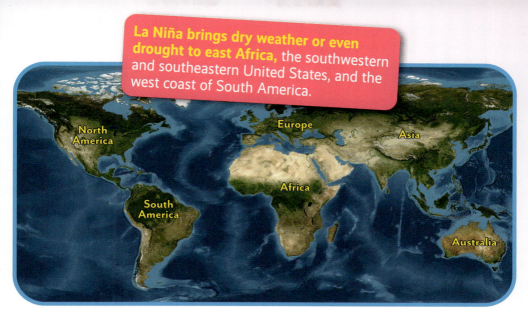

La Niña brings dry weather or even drought to east Africa, the southwestern and southeastern United States, and the west coast of South America.

Southern Africa, Australia, Southeast Asia, and much of the American West and Midwest are wetter than usual during La Niña.

During seasons with El Niños and La Niñas, migrating birds may end up in odd places, and diseases carried by mosquitoes may spread more easily.

El Niños and La Niñas usually happen every two to seven years. In between, weather patterns return to normal.

The Human Element

Natural shifts in weather, such as El Niño and La Niña, aren't the only cause of unusual heat and drought. Human activities also change weather patterns and make their effects more severe. The **fossil fuels** we burn to power our homes, businesses, and vehicles are raising temperatures worldwide. This heating leads to more frequent and severe heat waves and droughts. We are also harming our water supplies when we farm more and more land to get enough food to feed Earth's growing population.

Planting crops that require lots of water is turning more land dry.

When groundwater is gone, soil dries out and erodes, leading to worse droughts.

Since 2000, droughts have become three times more frequent. They also last three times longer.

Science to the Rescue

Even if you can do nothing to change the weather, it helps to be prepared. **Meteorologists** study rain and snow totals to compare them to long-term averages. They check soil moisture and water levels in streams and lakes. Satellites gather pressure, wind, moisture, and storm **data** from all over Earth. All this information helps these weather experts make **accurate** predictions about upcoming heat and drought dangers. Early warnings help everyone from farmers to families prepare for what's ahead.

Drones are collecting data to better predict and prepare for heat waves, droughts, and other severe weather.

Meteorologists predicts that all seasons will be hotter, with fewer cold spells going forward.

Be Prepared!

If meteorologists are able to give us an early warning about heat waves and drought, we can prepare to protect both our health and our natural resources. To save precious water, farmers can use better **irrigation** systems and plant drought-resistant crops. Businesses and homes can install toilets, showers, and faucets that use less water. Local governments, police and fire departments, and charity groups can set up cooling centers during heat waves and stock up on food and water in case of drought.

To create a reserve water supply, some people collect rainwater in barrels. It can then be used to water plants during droughts.

Satellites can help us spot where droughts may be starting and encourage those places to begin stocking up on food supplies.

IT LOOKS LIKE A DROUGHT IS STARTING IN ASIA. SEND A WARNING!

When a heat wave is in the forecast, hospitals gear up to treat heat sickness.

Green roofs—roofs that are completely covered in plants—**keep buildings cool naturally and put rainwater to good use.**

Modern toilets use much less water than those from the past. That's partly because some places made laws about how much water a toilet could use to flush.

25

A Cool Future

We can prepare ourselves for the worst effects of heat waves and droughts, but could we one day prevent some of them altogether? The more the planet heats up, the more likely we'll be to get severe weather. We can start now to stop future heat waves and droughts. Using clean solar, wind, and water energy will cut down on heat-trapping gases. So will driving cars and trucks powered by electricity instead of gas. By taking action, we can all work together for a cooler, wetter tomorrow!

Making new clothes, bottles, cans, and plastic containers takes a lot of fossil fuel. **Recycling old items uses less energy and produces less heat-trapping gases.**

DON'T FORGET TO TURN OFF THE WATER THIS TIME!

DON'T WORRY, I WON'T.

Turning off the faucet while you're brushing your teeth **saves as much as 8 gallons (30 L) of water a day!**

Grass needs a lot of water to stay green. Instead, cover your yard with **rocks, wood chips, and plants that don't need much watering.**

Make good gardening choices by choosing seeds or plants that don't need a lot of water.

Farmers can let grass grow tall in their pastures. It will keep the ground cool and moist on hot days.

Trees pull **carbon dioxide**, one of the biggest heat-trapping gases, out of the air. **So, planting trees is a natural way to cool the planet!**

Too Salty!

Activity

Much of Earth's fresh water is underground. We can tap into this source to water our food crops, but sometimes there's a hidden problem: salt. Ocean water can seep into groundwater near the coast, making it salty. Let's see what happens to crops in salty water.

Plants need a small amount of salt to survive, but too much salt can poison them.

What You Will Need
- Raw sunflower seeds
- A small bowl
- Water
- 2 small jars
- Potting soil
- 2 small containers
- Salt
- Masking tape
- A black marker

Chinese scientists have developed a special kind of rice. This seawater rice can grow in salty soil near the ocean.

Step One

Soak the sunflower seeds in water for about 10 hours.

Step Two

Fill two jars with soil. Plant three seeds just below the surface in each jar.

Step Three

Put your jars in a sunny spot. If the soil gets dry, add a little water. It should take about 10 days for sprouts to grow.

Step Four

Fill two containers with about ¼ cup of water each. Then, add 2 teaspoons of salt to one container. Use masking tape and a marker to label the salty container. Then, make another label for the plain water container. Label your jars with plants the same way.

Step Five

Water the salt water plant with the salt water and the other plant with plain water for two weeks. What happens to each plant?

Glossary

accurate free from mistakes

agricultural relating to farming

carbon dioxide a greenhouse gas given off when fossil fuels are burned

data information and facts, such as measurements

dehydrated not having enough water or other body fluids

erodes wears away

evaporates removes some of the water from something, often by heating it up

famine a severe shortage of food

fertile producing a lot of crops, plants, or trees

fossil fuels natural gas, coal, and oil formed from plant or animal remains

groundwater water within Earth that feeds springs and wells

heatstroke a sickness in which a person stops sweating, their body temperature rises, and they become exhausted

humid moist and damp

irrigation the watering of land using human-made systems

meteorological relating to the atmosphere, weather, and weather forecasting

meteorologists people who study the atmosphere, weather, and weather forecasting

vegetation plant life

Read More

Bergin, Raymond. *Warming Planet (What on Earth? Climate Change Explained).* Minneapolis: Bearport Publishing, 2022.

Klatte, Kathleen A. *Droughts (Rosen Verified: Natural Disasters).* Buffalo, New York: Rosen Publishing, 2023.

McGregor, Harriet. *Heat Wave Horror! (Uncharted: Stories of Survival).* Minneapolis: Bearport Publishing, 2021.

Learn More Online

1. Go to **www.factsurfer.com** or scan the QR code below.
2. Enter **"X-treme Heat and Droughts"** into the search box.
3. Click on the cover of this book to see a list of websites.

Index

clouds 6, 12, 17

crops 4, 15–17, 20, 24, 28

desert 14

Dust Bowl 16

El Niño 18–20

evaporation 10

famine 16

farmers 16, 22, 24, 27

farms 4, 20

fossil fuels 20, 26

groundwater 13, 20, 28

health 11, 24

heat sickness 25

La Niña 18–20

meteorologists 22–24

moisture 6, 10, 22

ocean 13, 18, 28

plants 12–13, 16, 20, 24–25, 27–29

precipitation 12–13, 15

pressure 6, 12, 18, 22

rain 4, 6, 12–14, 22

snow 5, 12, 22

soil 4, 12, 16–17, 20, 22, 28–29

sweat 10

temperature 6–10, 20–22

vegetation 16

water cycle 12, 14

About the Author

Marcia Abramson lives in Ann Arbor, Michigan. It has some dry spells and heat waves, but it also gets a lot of rain and snow.